FROM ······

Slave Ship

TO ······

Freedom Road

FROM Slave Ship TO Freedom Road

JULIUS LESTER

PAINTINGS BY ROD BROWN

Dial Books New York

In memory of the Old Ones
—J.L.

To my loving wife, Cathy, and
in memory of Diane Yevette Ritter, 1968-1995
—R.B.

Published by Dial Books
A Division of Penguin Books USA Inc.
375 Hudson Street
New York, New York 10014

Designed by Julie Rauer
Printed in Hong Kong on acid-free paper
First Edition
10 9 8 7 6 5 4 3 2 1

Library of Congress Cataloging in Publication Data
Lester, Julius.
From slave ship to freedom road / Julius Lester ; paintings by Rod Brown.
p. cm.
ISBN 0-8037-1893-4
1. Brown, Rod, date—Themes, motives. 2. Slavery in art. 3. Afro-Americans in art.
I. Brown, Rod, date. II. Title.
ND237.B8744A4 1998 759.13—dc21 96-44422 CIP

It has been almost thirty years since I wrote a book called *To Be a Slave*. In that work I sought to convey the slave experience by combining historical narrative and the personal narratives of those who had been slaves. In two subsequent works of fiction, *Long Journey Home* and *This Strange New Feeling*, I continued to explore the slave experience.

When presented with Rod Brown's paintings, I was jolted into the realization that perhaps I was not done with writing about what it was like to have been a slave. His work was a visceral response to slavery that eschewed photographic realism for a raw power that gave flesh to soul. What kind of text would be appropriate for such personal work? I thought of creating a historical narrative, or using the words of ex-slaves again. But the challenge was to meet the paintings at the depth of being from which they had been painted. This was one man's confrontation with the American slave experience and the lives of his ancestors. The words that emerged from me were also personal, words that spoke from yesterday's history and today's.

Even more surprising was the degree to which I found myself addressing you, the reader, begging, pleading, imploring you not to be passive, but to invest soul and imagine yourself into the images. Art and literature ask us to step out of our skins and put on the skins of others. Rod Brown and I ask of you what we asked of ourselves as we sought to come to terms with a historical experience whose legacy continues to affect us all.

Julius Lester

They took the sick and the dead *and dropped them into the sea like empty wine barrels. But wine barrels did not have beating hearts, crying eyes, and screaming mouths.*

I think often of those ancestors of mine whose names I do not know, whose names I will never know, those ancestors who saw people thrown into the sea like promises casually made and easily broken. It was primarily the youngest and strongest who survived the Middle Passage, that three-month-long ocean voyage from the western shores of Africa to the so-called New World. My ancestors might have been young when the slave ship left, but when it docked, they were haunted by memories of kinsmen tossed into the sea like promises never meant to be kept, and of gulls crying like mourners. They could still hear the wind wailing at the sight of black bodies bobbing in blue water like bottles carrying notes nobody would ever read.

So many Africans were thrown into the sea, sharks swam alongside slave ships, waiting for the inevitable bodies. From approximately 1518 until 1865, ships from Great Britain, Holland, Portugal, France, and the United States brought Africans to the New World to work for no money.

Millions were taken. No one knows how many millions died.

Except the sharks.

Side by side they lay: coffin straight, coffin narrow, coffin black.
Side by side they lay, alive, alive, oh so alive.

It is difficult to imagine times and places long past. We must try if we are to redeem those times and ourselves. The means by which we can do this is the imagination, which gives flesh and blood and soul to past—and present. Each of those millions of Africans was/is a story, just as you and I are stories.

VOICE ONE: *The darkness was blacker than any night. Where was my father? my mother? Did they know where I was? Why didn't they come and get me? Did they ever know what happened to me?*

VOICE TWO: *Our bodies did what they had to do where we lay. Urine and excrement fell on me from above, and mine onto those below. The smell was as thick as hatred.*

VOICE THREE: *I was shackled by my wrists and ankles to a man on my right and one on my left. I could not stand. I could not turn over. I will never understand what I did to deserve this.*

This is what I imagine three Africans might have said. What would it be like not to know where you were going, or what was going to happen to you when you got there?

You have memories of those Africans too. Even if you're white.

Especially if you're white.

Anger as hard as a mountain, Anger as wide as hatred
Anger as dense as night, Anger as long as ever

IMAGINATION EXERCISE ONE · For White People

It is a sunny day. Suddenly a spaceship lands and people of a skin color you have never seen come out of the ship and drag you aboard—you, your family, neighbors, and friends. The ship takes off and flies for three months. When it lands, you are in a place you never knew existed and the people speak a language you have never heard. They have weapons that hurt, maim, and kill. They give you a name—Mammy, Remus, Jemima, Sambo. They do not care what your real name is or who you really are. You are their slave and you exist now to work for them.

Imagine a rage so fierce it would scorch the earth, leaving behind only a giant cinder to circle the sun. You do not have to be black to be this angry. Your ancestors need not have been Africans. You need only wonder: How would I feel if that happened to me?

When we can imagine the hurt and anger of another, we have an understanding in the heart. When we understand in the heart, each of us is less alone.

Step right up! New shipment of niggers just in. These niggers are as black as Satan's thoughts, which means it don't matter how hot the sun gets, they will work like it's the cool of the day. However, they're so black, it's hard to see them in the dark. But don't worry. At night they bring out their banjos and drums. If you can't see 'em in the dark, you'll sure hear 'em.

Nigger. They called us'n that from our first cry to our last breath. It ain't nothing but a word, some might say, but words hurt like whips and they leave scars you can't see and what don't never heal. You might think that what hurt us slaves the most was the beatings. But there's lot worse than getting whupped.

Like the day they stood my sister Maggie on the auction block and tore her blouse so the white men could see her breasts and joke about how many babies them breasts could nurse. That hurt worse than a whupping. Or the day they stood me up there and undid my pants and exposed my privates. My little boy and girl was there and they saw. That hurt worse than a whupping.

My ol' massa thinks he knows me. But if he don't care to try and know what really hurts me, how can he ever know me?

Nine months after you buy one of these niggers, you will have a plantation full of nigger babies. These niggers are a bargain and I will start the bidding at a mere eight hundred dollars. Do I hear eight hundred? I have eight. Do I hear eight-fifty?

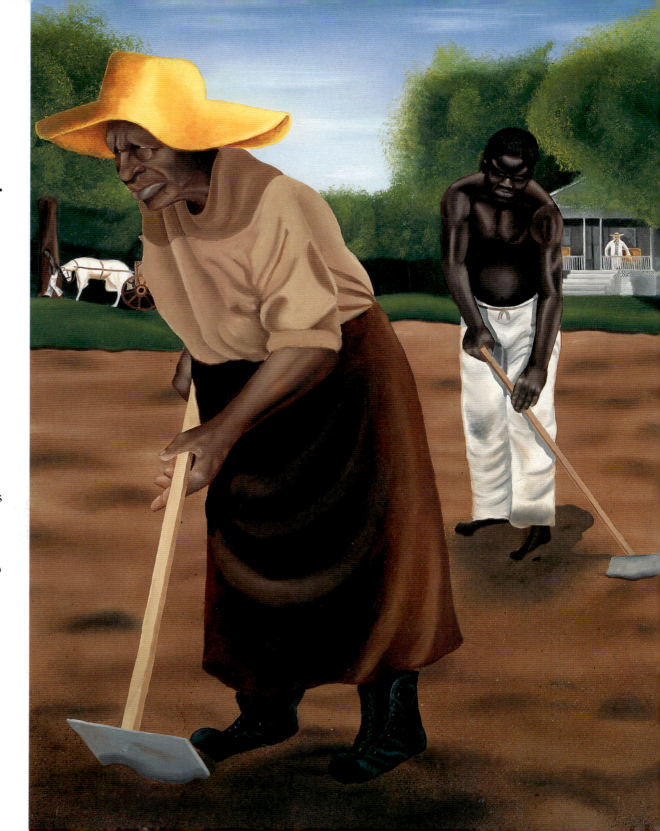

IMAGINATION EXERCISE TWO ·
For African Americans

Let's be honest, black people.
Many of us are ashamed that we are
descendants of slaves, aren't we?
Something inside us cringes at the
sight of these black women washing the
white man's clothes and hoeing the
white man's field. But what
if the shame is ours and not theirs?

Look at Mammy and Sarah Jane.
Look at the power in Mammy's shoulders
and arms. Look at her feet and how
solidly they rest upon the earth.
Look at her face. What do you see there?
Defiance? Anger? Self-possession?
Now look at Sarah Jane. She looks
resigned, but is she? You are free, but
are you?

My slave ancestors were house servants. Sometimes I jokingly say that my family was middle class even in slavery. After slavery my maternal great-grandmother, Maggie Carson, continued to serve tea and cookies every day at 4 o'clock, wearing the same black apron as she had in the master's house.

Who is more heroic?—slaves like Nat Turner, Sojourner Truth, and Frederick Douglass, who fought back, or an anonymous slave holding on to his hat as white as cotton. We do not have to choose. Heroism has many faces. One is finding the eternal in the ordinary and touching forever in the everyday.

Look! Look! A storm is coming! A storm like the one God is going to bring. God's wind is going to blow evil from this world as surely as this storm is going to scatter cotton over the ground. The rain is going to come down like the one God is going to send to purify this sinful world. And after the storm us'n will look into the sky and there yonder they'll be—chariots swinging low to hoist us up and carry us on away from here. Look! Look! A storm is coming!

When I was young, I liked to listen to old people talk about what things had been like when they were young. They would get a faraway look in their eyes and I knew they were seeing that faraway time called the past. I wanted their eyes to be mine so I could see what had been, so I could know what they knew.

Tibby looks as if he is more there than here. What do you think he is seeing? Or who? If you could ask him a question, what would it be?

I'd like to know how he got those holes in his hat and why doesn't he get a new one?

Go ahead. Close your eyes. Ask him a question. Then wait. If you are patient and listen closely, he will answer you.

My real name is Timothy and so was my son's. Folks called him Little Timmy. He couldn't say that. Most he could manage was Tibby. And that's what they started calling me. Massa sold Little Tibby when he was five years old. Just come and took him one day. That was fifty years ago. When you see me looking way off into the ever, I be hearing him calling to me as Massa took him away.

"Big Tibby! Big Tibby!"

That was the last time I saw him.

Running away was common. People ran because they had been mistreated or they were afraid they were going to be sold, or they just wanted to be free. Posters offering rewards for the capture of runaways were as much a part of the southern landscape as mosquito bites in the spring.

In North Carolina, slaves ran away to the mountains and were taken in by Cherokee Indians. Slaves from Georgia and Alabama disappeared into Florida, which until 1819 belonged to Spain and thus was outside the laws of the United States. The runaways joined with Seminole Indians and made forays back into Georgia and Alabama to free more slaves. In Virginia, slaves ran away and disappeared into a forbidding and almost impenetrable area called the Great Dismal Swamp. They lived there for decades, creating small villages of runaway slaves. Many slaves escaped to free states in the North, while others went farther north into Canada.

But for all those who ran away, most were caught and brought back by the white patrols, or "patterollers" as the slaves called them. They stumbled and fell as they were pulled and dragged by a rope tied to a horse's saddle horn. They were brought back to be made examples of, so the other slaves could see what would happen to them if they tried to escape. For some, dying in the effort to be free was better than being a slave. Samuel got caught. It didn't mean Samuel wouldn't try again. And again. And again.

The sound of the whip
ripping black flesh,
Screams tearing still air.
Then, silence and the sound
of our own breath-starved
Screaming.

IMAGINATION EXERCISE THREE · For Whites and Blacks

I am tempted to ask you to imagine the pain and suffering of slaves such as these who were beaten unmercifully, slaves who were murdered. But that is too easy. We know slavery was cruel and we are ready, even eager, to lather sympathy on the poor slaves.

So I will ask something more difficult. Imagine not the victim, but the aggressor.

We may think that we would never whip someone until their flesh cried blood. But what if you would not be punished for doing it? What if your peers approved and deemed you honorable and good for beating someone? What then?

Evil is as mesmerizing as a snake's eyes. Though difficult, we must imagine our capacity for evil.

Unless and until we do, unseen shadows of hung men will blot the walls of our homes.

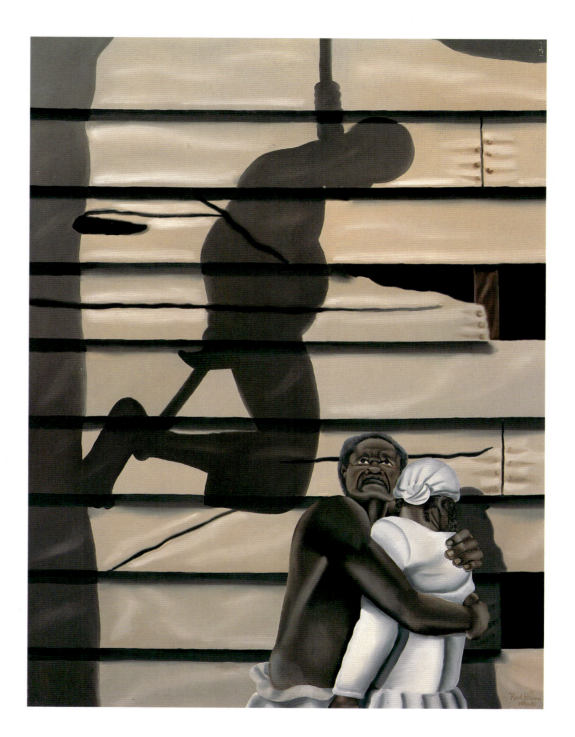

Who am I? What is my place in the scheme of things? We want our lives to have meaning and importance. Imagine seeking the meaning of your life if you had been a slave. The white preachers said you were cursed by God to serve white people even in heaven. But what kind of God was that? you wondered. Didn't that holy book of the white folks say everybody was made in God's image? And that meant God looked like you too.

Late at night you went deep into the woods and prayed to that God who looked like you, asking him to remember you as he had remembered the children of Israel.

Didn't my Lord deliver Daniel
Deliver Daniel
Deliver Daniel
Didn't my Lord deliver Daniel
Then why not every man?

Afro-American Spiritual

All of us need to understand who we are and what our place is in the scheme of things. Through stories we alight on the meaning and significance of our lives.

To control their slaves the slaveowners and preachers knew they had to strip them of their individual and cultural identities. Slaves should have no other stories than the ones their owners told them.

But despite this the slaves also told stories to each other. What story is the old man telling the children? Why are some of the children grinning? Whose story are the children becoming? Whose stories are you?

To have value in the heart of another. To value another in your heart. Is that not what it means to be human? If I value you in my heart, I would rather hurt myself than hurt you. If I value you in my heart.

Slavery was part of a business. The slaveowner wanted to make as much money as he could. But what happened if the price of cotton fell one year and the slaveowner could not pay his bills? He would have to raise cash and cut expenses. A slave was an expense like mules, horses, plows, and cottonseed.

"John, I'm sorry but I'm going to have to sell Delilah."

"Oh, Massa, you can't do that! She's the only child we got left."

"I don't have any choice. She's young and she'll bring a good price on the market. You understand how it is. Things have been bad this year what with the drought and the market being flooded with Egyptian cotton. If I don't sell off some of the slaves, I'll lose everything."

"You sell my daughter, Massa, and I lose everything."

"I'm sorry, John. I really am."

Slavery was a business. Sometimes people had to be sold to keep the business going. That's how it is if you want to make a profit.

For slaves trying to escape, there were no Rand McNally maps with routes marked "This way to freedom." There were no interstate highways with rest stops. But there was moss growing on the north side of trees, and the shadows of trees falling west or north, and at night the North Star. And there were always rivers to cross.

How did they manage that? Who knows? Runaway slaves were careful not to tell the secrets of how they escaped, fearing they would deprive other slaves of using the same methods. How do you cross a river when you can't take the ferry or walk over a bridge?

But crossing a river was minor compared to making the decision to escape. There are many more fears than there are rivers, and fears are harder to wade through.

What if we get caught?

What if somebody gets hurt or dies along the way?

How will we eat?

What if we make it to freedom? Then what?

Where will we live? How will we make a living?

The only way to cross over fear is to do what you are afraid of doing.

Throughout slavery there were white people who risked their lives to help runaway slaves. They believed the best way to affirm their humanity was to fight against slavery. Some even died. Most were ordinary people who made secret rooms in their homes where runaway slaves could hide as they made their way north along that network known as the Underground Railroad. So many whites and free blacks began to assist runaways that the federal government passed a law—the Fugitive Slave Act of 1850—making it illegal to help runaway slaves. This made many hate slavery even more.

Why did these people—and whites in particular—risk their freedom and safety to help runaway slaves? Would you risk going to jail to help someone you didn't know? Would you risk losing your freedom to help someone not of your race?

Many who took such risks did so because they believed it was the right thing to do. They had studied the Bible and sat in church Sunday after Sunday. To them it was obvious. God was on the side of the poor and the oppressed. If they were going to do God's work, they had to help the poor and the oppressed.

It was just that simple.

The history books say Abraham Lincoln freed the slaves. It is true that he signed a document called the Emancipation Proclamation, which established the legal precedent for freedom. But to give all the credit to Lincoln omits what the slaves and free blacks did for themselves—and the nation.

Ultimately, no one can free anyone else. You have to free yourself. Somebody else can unlock the door and even push it ajar, but they can't walk through it for you. You have to do that.

That's how it was when the Civil War started in 1861, the war that would determine whether America was going to be one nation devoid of slavery or two nations, one for slaveowners and slaves and the other for free people.

Blacks, slave and free, knew it would not be good if only white men risked their lives on the battlefields. It would not be good if only white men lost arms, legs, and their lives while black men stood on the sidelines, unmaimed, unhurt, alive. Slaves ran away from plantations in droves whenever the Union Army came near, begging to be used in the war effort. In the North, free blacks led by the ex-slave orator Frederick Douglass beseeched the government to let them join the army. Douglass became the first black man to ever meet with a U. S. president when he sat down with Lincoln and urged him to create an all-black regiment to fight in the war. Finally Lincoln agreed.

The war to end slavery could only accomplish its purpose if those most directly affected fought and died too. And they did.

What was it like to dream about freedom, long for freedom, and never dare hope that it would happen? Then one day, a day like all the other days, you're working in the field. You see a Union soldier dressed in blue ride up to the slaveowner's house. A little later he and the slaveowner come to the field and tell you to stop working because the slaveowner has something to tell you.

"You're free," he says. "I don't own you no more. You can come and go as you please, just like a white man."

What would you feel?

Look at the slaves. Look at their faces. What do you see there? You would think they would be happy. Why do they look apprehensive and afraid?

Freedom from slavery was not the same as freedom to do whatever they wanted. They were free, but where were they supposed to go? They owned no land. They had no houses of their own. What were they supposed to do with this freedom if they did not have money or a place to live?

Free, free! They were free! I have no doubt that inside themselves, freed slaves were delirious with excitement. But on the outside they did not know what freedom meant. Some slaveowners kicked their former slaves off the land. Others allowed their ex-slaves to remain and work for money; the former slaveowners still needed their labor and the former slaves needed jobs.

Many slaves stayed where they were. Others left, not knowing where they were going and not much caring. Still others went in search of wives and children and husbands who had been sold away.

Freedom. To be responsible for oneself and one's time.

Freedom. To own oneself.

Freedom. To be one's own master.

Freedom. It's like a promise we are still learning how to keep.

LIST OF PAINTINGS

Water Passage (front cover and p. 31), 30″ x 40″, private collection of Velma Clay; *Last Chain to Break* (p. 2), 30″ x 40″,

private collection of Velma Clay; *Bodies in the Sea* (p. 7), 24″ x 36″; *Sheol* (p. 8), 24″ x 36″, private collection of Vivian Ritter; *Souls of*

Bondage (p. 11), 30″ x 40″, private collection of Steven Lewis; *Nubian Nation* (p. 13), 24″ x 48″, private collection of Velma Clay;

Mammy (p. 14), 30″ x 40″; *Toils of Sarah Jane* (p. 15), 30″ x 40″; *Ah Storm's Ah Comin* (p. 16), 30″ x 40″; *Tibby—Portrait of a*

Slave (p. 19), 30″ x 40″, private collection; *Samuel's Return* (p. 20), 24″ x 48″; *Luther's Beating* (p. 22), 24″ x 48″; *Murder of Niggah*

Charlie (p. 23), 30″ x 40″; *Massa's Gospel* (p. 24), 30″ x 40″, private collection of Kenneth Kave; *In the Spirit* (p. 25), 24″ x 36″;

The Griot (p. 26), 24″ x 36″; *Lord Not My Child* (p. 29), 24″ x 36″, private collection of Mattie Freedman; *Friends of Freedom* (p. 32),

24″ x 48″; *My Brother, My Brother* (p. 34), 24″ x 36″; *Then Came the Word* (p. 37), 24″ x 48″, private collection of Vivian Ritter;

Goodbye Mississippi Autumn (p. 39), 24″ x 48″; *Leaving the South* (back cover), 24″ x 36″.

These paintings, along with others by Rod Brown, have been exhibited in several museums and shows under the

title "From Slavery to Freedom."